PICNICS IN THE PARK

MOVEABLE FEASTS
FOR DINING ALFRESCO

BY CONNIE MCCOLE

ILLUSTRATIONS BY CYNTHIA FITTING

HEARST BOOKS
NEW YORK

For my mom, with love

〜

To Jim, Christopher, and Ryan: thanks for making it happen again.

Compilation copyright © 1993 by Fly Productions
Text copyright © 1993 by Connie McCole
Illustrations copyright © 1993 by Cynthia Fitting

It is the policy of William Morrow and Company, Inc., and its imprints and affiliates, recognizing the importance of preserving what has been written, to print the books we publish on acid-free paper, and we exert our best efforts to that end.

Library of Congress Cataloging-in-Publication Data

McCole, Connie.
Picnics in the park : moveable feasts for dining alfresco /
by Connie McCole ; illustrations by Cynthia Fitting. — 1st ed.
p. cm.
ISBN 0-688-11823-2
1. Outdoor cookery. 2. Picnicking. I. Title
TX 823.M353 1993

641.5'784—dc20   92-36352
                                                            CIP

Printed in Singapore

First Edition

1 3 5 7 9 10 8 6 4 2

F🦟Y
PRODUCTIONS

Contents

INTRODUCTION

Dining outdoors is one of life's great pleasures. Surely, there's no finer tradition than sharing your picnic basket with a friend. The winter doldrums are cast aside along with social conventions. Proper picnic etiquette lets you kick off your shoes, eat with your fingers, and recline while you dine.

Picnics are a ritual enjoyed the world over. Whenever I'm on vacation, I explore the local food stores or farmers' markets, buying a little bit of this and a little bit of that to feel closer to the people and the places I'm visiting. I return home eager to recapture their singular ambience and re-create all the memorable dishes I've discovered. I share my favorites here, to be enjoyed whether you're actually soaking up the sun in Barcelona's incredible Güell Park, or only wish you were. The ten easy-to-prepare menus in this book will show you how to capture the essence of one wonderful alfresco destination after another.

Because your adventure will be more free-spirited with some forward planning, "The Day Before" section of every menu describes preparations that can be made in advance. As you can see from the estimated preparation times for "The Day Before" and "Picnic Day," very little remains to be done on the morning of your picnic — brewing a tea, perhaps, or simply packing up the dishes already prepared. All of these perfectly portable meals serve two. Each menu also includes serving suggestions — special touches that will give you a sense of being there, even if you're not so very far from home.

So pack your basket with a picnic banquet and escape to an elegant holiday in London's Hyde Park, a lazy intermezzo in Rome's Borghese Gardens, or a rustic barbecue under Montana's big sky. Whatever your destination, a neighborhood park or right in your own backyard, an outdoor dining adventure awaits you.

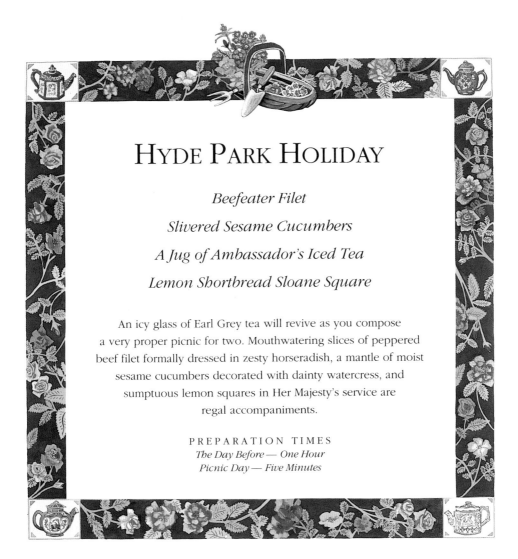

Hyde Park Holiday

Beefeater Filet

Slivered Sesame Cucumbers

A Jug of Ambassador's Iced Tea

Lemon Shortbread Sloane Square

An icy glass of Earl Grey tea will revive as you compose
a very proper picnic for two. Mouthwatering slices of peppered
beef filet formally dressed in zesty horseradish, a mantle of moist
sesame cucumbers decorated with dainty watercress, and
sumptuous lemon squares in Her Majesty's service are
regal accompaniments.

PREPARATION TIMES
The Day Before — One Hour
Picnic Day — Five Minutes

1

THE DAY BEFORE

Prepare the Beefeater Filet: Arrange the cooled beef slices on a platter, cover, and refrigerate overnight. Wash and dry the watercress, roll in paper towels, and refrigerate in a plastic bag. Place the blended horseradish sauce in a covered container and refrigerate overnight.

Prepare the Sesame Cucumbers: Toss the cucumbers in the sesame dressing. Cover and refrigerate overnight.

Prepare the Iced Tea: Refrigerate in a covered pitcher overnight.

Prepare the Lemon Shortbread: Bake the shortbread. Let it sit, uncovered, at room temperature overnight.

Assemble the Picnic Basket: A wicker hamper and a tartan traveling rug are must-haves. Pack flatware, including steak knives (sterling, naturally), white linen napkins piped in purple, and Victorian dinner plates. Have a thermos on hand to transport your very Yankee iced tea.

BEEFEATER FILET

1 tablespoon black peppercorns
1 teaspoon kosher salt
One 8-ounce filet of beef, about 1 1/2 inches thick
1/4 cup sour cream
2 teaspoons prepared white horseradish
Small bunch watercress

In a mini-food processor or spice grinder, coarsely grind the peppercorns

and salt. Scatter the seasoning on a dinner plate. Press the beef into the ground salt and pepper to coat well on both sides. Lift the filet off the plate and press again, with the side of your fist, to ensure that the seasonings are well affixed. Set aside to allow the spices to permeate the meat, about forty-five minutes.

Preheat the oven to 400°F. Place the seasoned filet in a small heavy roasting dish. Roast for four to six minutes per side for medium-rare, turning the filet once. Cool for about ten minutes before slicing into thin strips.

In a small bowl, thoroughly combine the sour cream and horseradish, adjusting the horseradish to taste.

Slivered Sesame Cucumbers

Peel one cucumber. Cut it in half lengthwise and remove the seeds. Slice into thin half-moons. Toss the slices in a dressing made from two tablespoons freshly squeezed lemon juice, one tablespoon sesame oil, and salt and freshly ground black pepper to taste.

A Jug of Ambassador's Iced Tea

Boil one quart of water. Add four Earl Grey tea bags and remove the pan from the heat. Brew the tea for five minutes. Remove the tea bags. Add one-quarter cup sugar, five tablespoons freshly squeezed lemon juice (the juice of about two lemons), and the lemon rinds. When cool, pour into a pitcher.

On the day of the picnic, remove the rinds and discard.

Lemon Shortbread Sloane Square

1 1/4 cups all-purpose flour
1/4 cup confectioners' sugar
4 ounces unsalted butter, softened
2 large eggs
1 cup granulated sugar
1/4 teaspoon baking powder
3 tablespoons freshly squeezed lemon juice
Grated rind of 1 lemon

In a large bowl or food processor, combine one cup of flour, confectioners' sugar, and butter until a ball of dough forms. Press into the bottom of an eight-inch square ovenproof dish. Refrigerate for fifteen minutes. Heat the oven to 350°F. Bake until lightly golden, about twelve minutes.

In a large bowl, combine the eggs, granulated sugar, baking powder, lemon juice, lemon rind, and remaining flour. Mix until smooth. Pour the mixture onto the warm crust. Bake until a toothpick inserted comes out clean, twenty to twenty-five minutes. Cool in the pan, then cut into sixteen two-inch squares.

Picnic Spread English Style

Place your settings just-so, with napkins crisply folded and silver shining. On each plate, nestle some cucumbers beside a bed of watercress moistened with dressing. Fan the beef slices, drizzling on the zesty horseradish.

Sonoma Savor

Vintner's Wild Rice Salad

Roasted Asparagus with A Citrus Vinaigrette

Valley of the Moon Chocolate Raspberry Torte

Sonoma County Sauvignon Blanc

Heady with the scent of grapes ripening on the vine, the heart of California's wine country inspires a picnic feast. A chilled Sauvignon Blanc, selected during your morning's tour of the vineyards, is just right for a lovely lunch of crisp-roasted asparagus seasoned with orange vinaigrette, a flavorful wild rice salad tossed with regional specialties, and a sliver of torte, sinfully rich.

PREPARATION TIMES
The Day Before — One Hour Plus
Picnic Day — Five Minutes

The Day Before

Prepare the Wild Rice Salad: Toss all the ingredients with the cooked wild rice. Cover and refrigerate overnight.

Prepare the Roasted Asparagus: Dress the roasted spears with the cirtus vinaigrette. Cover and refrigerate overnight.

Prepare the Chocolate Raspberry Torte: Bake the torte. Allow it to sit, uncovered, at room temperature overnight.

Assemble the Picnic Basket: Fold your flatware into grape-pattern napkins tied in place with gold satin bows. Blue-and-white spongeware dishes with matching salad bowl, vegetable platter, and cake plate will conjure the scudding clouds of a perfect Northern California sky. Include two wineglasses, a corkscrew, and a cake knife, too.

Vintner's Wild Rice Salad

2/3 cup wild rice
6 ounces thickly sliced smoked chicken, cut in 1/2-inch cubes
4 ounces white mushrooms, cleaned and cut in sixths
1/3 cup walnuts, coarsely chopped
2/3 cup seedless grapes, quartered
1/2 cup mayonnaise
Salt and freshly ground black pepper to taste

Boil two cups of water in a medium saucepan. Add the wild rice, cover, and turn the heat to low. Cook until just tender, thirty-five to forty minutes. Drain the rice in a colander and allow to cool. Place in a large bowl and toss with the smoked chicken, mushrooms, walnuts, and grapes. Add the mayonnaise and combine well. Taste for salt and pepper.

ROASTED ASPARAGUS WITH A CITRUS VINAIGRETTE

Preheat the oven to 500°F. In a small bowl, whisk one-quarter cup of olive oil, the grated rind of one small orange, two teaspoons freshly squeezed orange juice, one tablespoon raspberry vinegar, and salt and freshly ground black pepper to taste. Set the citrus vinaigrette aside. Trim and peel one pound asparagus. Place a single layer in a shallow baking dish. Lightly drizzle olive oil over all. Cook until the stalks are crisp-tender, six to eight minutes. Bite into one to test for doneness. Transfer to a vegetable dish. Drizzle over the citrus vinaigrette to coat the warm asparagus.

VALLEY OF THE MOON CHOCOLATE RASPBERRY TORTE

One 10-ounce package frozen raspberries in syrup, defrosted
4 ounces unsalted butter, at room temperature
6 ounces bittersweet or semisweet chocolate, melted and cooled
     to room temperature
2/3 cup granulated sugar
3 eggs
1/2 cup cake flour, sifted
Confectioners' sugar for dusting

Press the raspberries through a sieve or use a food mill fitted with a small disk. Place the raspberry juice in a small saucepan and boil until it reduces to about one-half cup of syrup, about seven minutes. Set aside to cool.

Preheat the oven to 350°F. Butter a nine-inch round cake pan and dust it with flour. Line the bottom with parchment.

Using an electric mixer, or by hand in a large bowl, beat the butter until pale and creamy. Add the chocolate and sugar. Beat until the mixture is fluffy, two to three minutes. Beat in the eggs, one at a time. Beat in the raspberry syrup, and then the flour. Beat until the mixture is *just* combined. Pour the batter into the prepared pan and bake until a toothpick inserted in the center comes out clean, twenty-five to thirty minutes. Let the torte cool in the pan for thirty minutes. Invert it onto a cooling rack to cool completely.

On the day of the picnic, dust the top with confectioners' sugar.

Picnic Spread California Style

Gather vibrant wildflowers to decorate your feast: Slip California poppies through the beribboned napkins. Accent your dishes with edible nasturtiums and Johnny-jump-ups. Within easy reach is the bowl brimming with wild rice salad, the roasted asparagus arranged on the vegetable platter, and the sugar-dusted torte framed by two proud glasses of Sonoma's finest Sauvignon Blanc.

Imperial Palace Banquet

Kyoto Lunchbox:

Soba Noodles with Wasabi and Baby Corn,

Oshi Tashi Spinach, and Edo Roasted Eggplant

Apple Pears and Green Tea

A lunchbox composition of delicate edibles is the art of Japanese dining outdoors. Tiny corn and zingy ginger lace each sharp-and-spicy helping of cold buckwheat noodles. The smoky medley of roasted eggplant and crunchy onions is deliciously complemented by health-giving sesame spinach. Balanced flavors of warming green tea and stimulating apple pears are the Buddha's glory.

PREPARATION TIMES
The Day Before— One Hour Plus
Picnic Day— Ten Minutes

11

The Day Before

Prepare the Soba Noodles: Toss the noodles with all the other ingredients. Divide into two equal portions, pack in the lunchbox, and refrigerate overnight.

Prepare the Oshi Tashi Spinach: Dress the spinach with the sesame sauce. Divide into two equal portions, pack in the lunchbox, and refrigerate overnight.

Prepare the Roasted Eggplant: Bake and sauce the eggplant. Divide into two equal portions, pack in the lunchbox, and refrigerate overnight.

Prepare the Apple Pears: Wash two Japanese apple pears and pat them dry. Store in a paper bag at room temperature overnight.

Assemble the Picnic Basket: Select two pretty lunchboxes, called _obento_, to present your picnic banquet Japanese style. These lacquered lunchboxes are designed for transporting your savories to the picnic site — and for slurping the delicious contents directly from the box when you get there. Each dish has its own self-contained compartment. Remember to bind two pottery mugs in ikat cotton napkins and pack it all in a bamboo basket, along with a matching tablecloth, two pairs of chopsticks, and a pair of chopstick rests. You'll also need a paring knife for slicing the pears.

Soba Noodles with Wasabi and Baby Corn

1 tablespoon black sesame seeds
1 tablespoon white sesame seeds
6 ounces soba (buckwheat noodles)
1/4 teaspoon wasabi (green horseradish) paste
2 tablespoons soy sauce
2 tablespoons sesame oil
2 tablespoons peanut oil
2 tablespoons balsamic vinegar
2 small garlic cloves, peeled and pressed
One 8-ounce jar baby corn, rinsed
4 green onions, green tops included, thinly sliced
1 tablespoon Japanese pickled ginger

Dry-toast the black and white sesame seeds in a heavy skillet over low heat, stirring occasionally, about fifteen minutes.

In a large pot of salted water, boil the soba noodles until they are al dente, about seven minutes. Drain and transfer to a large bowl.

In a small glass bowl, stir to combine the wasabi and the soy sauce. Set aside for ten minutes to allow the flavors to develop. Stir in the sesame and peanut oils, vinegar, and garlic. Diagonally slice each tiny corn cob in half. Toss the corn into the dressing and set aside to allow the flavors to blend, about fifteen minutes. Pour the corn-spiked dressing over the noodles and toss thoroughly to coat. Sprinkle on the green onions and pickled ginger and toss again gently.

Oshi Tashi Spinach

Trim and carefully wash one bunch (about one pound) of spinach. In a medium pot with several inches of boiling water, just *wilt* the spinach, about twenty seconds. Drain and refresh under cold water. Squeeze as much water out of the spinach as you can. Shred into strips, three inches long and one-half inch wide. Set aside in a medium bowl.

Dry-toast two tablespoons white sesame seeds in a heavy skillet over medium-low heat until they are lightly browned, about five minutes. In a mini-food processor or with a mortar and pestle, grind the seeds to a paste. Transfer to a small bowl and add four teaspoons soy sauce and one teaspoon sugar. Stir to dissolve. Pour over the spinach and toss gently.

Edo Roasted Eggplant

Preheat the oven to 400°F. Trim one pound of Japanese eggplants and cut lengthwise into quarters. Place in a baking dish, cut side down. Scatter over two small sliced onions, two minced garlic cloves, and two teaspoons minced fresh ginger. Drizzle one-third cup peanut oil over all. Season the eggplant with salt and freshly ground black pepper to taste. Bake on the top shelf of the oven until the eggplant can be pierced with a fork, about thirty-five minutes. Remove the dish from the oven to cool for five minutes. Drizzle two-and-one-half tablespoons rice wine vinegar over all. Sprinkle over salt and pepper to taste and top with two tablespoons chopped fresh cilantro.

GREEN TEA

On the day of the picnic, fill a teapot and a thermos with boiling water and set aside. Bring three cups of water to a brisk boil. Empty the teapot and add four teaspoons Japanese green tea leaves. Pour the boiling water over the tea leaves, cover, and steep for three or four minutes. Discard the water warming the thermos, strain the tea into the thermos, and you are ready to transport piping hot tea to your picnic.

PICNIC SPREAD JAPANESE STYLE

Spread your picnic near a flowering tree in full bloom; maybe a light breeze will send some petals fluttering down to decorate the tablecloth. Fold your napkins into origami lotus. Place the chopsticks on their rests beside each lacquer lunchbox. Your companion will be delighted to remove the lid and discover the treats hidden inside. The lunchbox tops will serve a fan of sliced apple pears to consume barbarian style — with your fingers.

LUXEMBOURG BONNE BOUCHE

La Coupole Charcuterie Plate

Lentil Salad with Chèvre

Leeks and Olives Jardinière

Palettes des Dames Cookies

Celebrate the romance of springtime in Paris with a classic French *pique-nique.* Your favorite pâtés and spicy meats are complemented by herbed lentil salad, spiked tangy with goat cheese, and saucy leeks vinaigrette. For a *déjeuner sur l'herbe* picnic as picture perfect as Manet's masterpiece, sip a young Beaujolais and nibble orange-liqueur cookies.

PREPARATION TIMES
The Day Before — One Hour
Picnic Day — Five Minutes

The Day Before

For the Charcuterie Plate: Select a variety of your favorite French picnic specialties — a slice of pâté de campagne, a wedge of duck rillettes, garlic-spiced saucisson rolled in black pepper, and paper-thin slices of jambon de Bayonne. Wrap your bounty in waxed paper and store in the refrigerator overnight. On the day of the picnic, slice the saucisson into bite-size wafers and buy a fresh baguette to ensure crusty goodness.

Prepare the Lentil Salad: Toss the cooked lentils in the marinade. Cover and refrigerate overnight. Wash and dry the lettuce, roll in paper towels, place in a plastic bag, and refrigerate overnight.

Prepare the Leeks and Olives Jardinière: Marinate the leeks overnight, covered and refrigerated.

Prepare the Palettes des Dames Cookies: Bake the cookies. Store in an airtight container at room temperature overnight.

Assemble the Picnic Basket: Flowery plates with matching napkins, a blue-and-white bistro tablecloth, and silver service for two tied with jaunty French wire ribbons are de rigeur. Remember, two pretty platters: one to display the delicious deli delicacies and another, topped with a doily, for the dainty cookies. A crock of whole-grain Dijon mustard and a jar of cornichons will give a savory smack to the charcuterie. Raise two red wineglasses to *la vie bohème.*

Lentil Salad with Chevre

4 garlic cloves, peeled
1 cup lentils, cleaned and rinsed
1/2 teaspoon salt
1 carrot, peeled and finely minced
1 small onion, peeled and finely minced
1 stalk celery, finely minced
1/2 cup extra-virgin olive oil
3 sprigs parsley, finely minced
4 ounces chèvre cheese
2 1/2 tablespoons red wine vinegar
Freshly ground black pepper and salt to taste
2 large butter lettuce leaves

With the back of a soup spoon, lightly crush two of the garlic cloves. Place in a medium saucepan with the lentils and salt. Cover with one inch of cold water. Bring to a boil. Lower the heat and simmer for ten minutes. Add the carrot, onion, and celery. Simmer until the lentils are tender-firm, about twenty-five minutes. Add a bit more water, if necessary, to prevent the lentils from scorching.

Using a slotted spoon, mound the cooked lentils on a cookie sheet. Toss with one-quarter cup of the olive oil. Spread the mixture to speed cooling.

Mince the two remaining garlic cloves. Place the cooled lentils, the parsley, and minced garlic in a large bowl. Crumble in the chèvre. Add the remaining olive oil, vinegar, and a few hearty twists of the pepper mill. Toss thoroughly. Taste the mixture and add more oil, vinegar, salt, or pepper if you choose.

At the picnic site, serve a dollop of lentils cupped in a lettuce leaf.

LEEKS AND OLIVES JARDINIERE

4 leeks, preferably thin
1/4 cup extra-virgin olive oil
1 teaspoon Dijon mustard
1 tablespoon red wine vinegar
1 tablespoon pitted Niçoise olives, minced
Salt and freshly ground black pepper to taste

Trim the leeks, leaving an inch or so of green. Wash carefully to remove grit. Gather into a bundle and tie with string. Place in a medium saucepan and cover with cold water. Bring to a boil, then lower the heat, and simmer until tender, about twelve minutes. Rinse in cold water and drain.

In a small bowl, whisk the olive oil, mustard, vinegar, olives, salt, and pepper to taste. Spoon the dressing over the leeks to coat nicely.

PALETTES DES DAMES COOKIES

4 tablespoons unsalted butter, at room temperature
1/2 cup confectioners' sugar
1/4 cup cake flour, plus 4 teaspoons

1/4 cup all-purpose flour
1 large egg white
2 tablespoons Grand Marnier
1/3 cup golden raisins

With a wooden spoon or paddle attachment of an electric mixer, beat the butter in a mixing bowl until smooth. Gradually beat in the sugar, all the cake flour, the all-purpose flour, egg white, and Grand Marnier until the batter is smooth. Fold in the raisins.

Preheat the oven to 325°F. Lightly grease two cookie sheets and dust with flour. Spoon rounded tablespoons of the batter onto the sheets. You will have enough for about eighteen cookies. Leave about two inches between each spoonful to allow the cookies to spread. Bake until the edges are golden, twelve to fifteen minutes. Transfer to a cooling rack.

PICNIC SPREAD FRENCH STYLE

Breathe the Beaujolais in the fragrant shade of a plum tree. Create a mouth-watering arrangement of charcuterie, with cornichons dancing in attendance, and a crock of mustard within spoon's reach. On each dinner plate, place two leeks and a lettuce cup filled with scrumptious lentil salad. Display the Palettes des Dames Cookies *à la pyramide* to munch later.

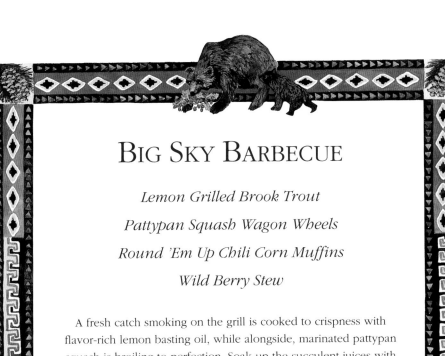

BIG SKY BARBECUE

Lemon Grilled Brook Trout

Pattypan Squash Wagon Wheels

Round 'Em Up Chili Corn Muffins

Wild Berry Stew

A fresh catch smoking on the grill is cooked to crispness with
flavor-rich lemon basting oil, while alongside, marinated pattypan
squash is broiling to perfection. Soak up the succulent juices with
the peppery zing of western-style chili corn muffins.
A ballad of berries is a sweet finale to a picnic
spread under Montana's big sky.

PREPARATION TIMES
The Day Before — One Hour
Picnic Day — Ten Minutes

The Day Before

For the Lemon Trout: In a small glass bowl, prepare a lemon-infused basting oil. Whisk one-third cup light olive oil, the grated zest of one lemon, two teaspoons minced lemon thyme, and a dash of salt. Cover and refrigerate overnight. Wrap two whole, cleaned trout in plain paper, place in plastic bags, and refrigerate overnight.

For the Pattypan Squash: Prepare the marinade in a nonmetallic bowl. Whisk all the ingredients together, except the squash and chopped tomatoes. Store the tomatoes separately, covered in a glass bowl. Refrigerate overnight. Parboil the squash, about two minutes. Drain and then plunge them into a bowl of cold water. Pat dry and slice each squash in half to make eight wagon-wheel rounds. Place in the marinade. Toss well to coat. Cover and refrigerate overnight.

Prepare the Chili Corn Muffins: Bake the muffins. Let them sit, covered, at room temperature overnight.

Prepare the Wild Berry Stew: Cook to combine all of the ingredients. Cover and refrigerate overnight.

Assemble the Picnic Basket: Pack your "saddlebag" with campfire-classic enamel dishes, matching coffee mugs, and a Native American blanket to lounge on — it will double as your tablecloth. Include the grilling utensils, an oversized spatula, and a basting brush. Wine goblets to serve the berry stew make a lovely presentation. Carry brewed java-for-two in a canteen to keep it steaming. At high noon, reach for horn-handled flatware, rolled smartly in colorful bandanas and tied with raffia lassos.

Lemon Grilled Brook Trout

Prepare a grill of medium-hot coals. Brush the outsides of both trout with lemon basting oil. Broil for about four minutes on each side, basting regularly to guarantee sealed-in flavor and moistness.

Pattypan Squash Wagon Wheels

6 tablespoons extra-virgin olive oil
2 tablespoons champagne vinegar
1 small shallot, peeled and minced
1 small garlic clove, peeled and minced
1 small serrano chili, minced
4 tablespoons chopped fresh basil
1/4 teaspoon salt
1/8 teaspoon freshly ground black pepper
4 pattypan squash, trimmed
2 medium tomatoes, chopped

Remove the seasoned squash wheels from the marinade. Toss in the tomatoes and reserve for later.

Arrange the squash on the grill to cook alongside the trout. Broil about four minutes on each side. When the squash is lightly browned and crisp-tender, place in the herbed tomato marinade and toss gently to coat.

Round 'Em Up Chili Corn Muffins

1/2 cup yellow cornmeal
1/2 cup all-purpose flour
1 tablespoon sugar
1 teaspoon baking powder
1/2 teaspoon salt
1/4 teaspoon baking soda
1/2 cup sour cream
1 extra-large egg
2 tablespoons unsalted butter, melted
2 ounces canned mild green chilies, chopped

Preheat the oven to 425°F. Generously grease six muffin cups. In a small bowl, mix the cornmeal, flour, sugar, baking powder, salt, and baking soda. In a large bowl, thoroughly combine the sour cream, egg, and melted butter. Add the dry ingredients to the mixture and stir until evenly moistened. Don't overmix the batter or the muffins will be tough. Fold in the chilies. Spoon the batter into the prepared cups, filling them to the top. Bake until a light golden color and a toothpick inserted in the center comes out clean, thirteen to eighteen minutes. Transfer to a cooling rack. When the muffins are cooled, wrap them in foil.

WILD BERRY STEW

Place one-and-one-half cups of blackberries and one-and-one-half cups raspberries in a nonaluminum pot. Add one-half cup cold water. Cover the pot and bring to a boil. Lower the heat slightly to gently boil the berries, about three minutes. Add one-half cup light brown sugar, three tablespoons granulated sugar, and a dash of salt. Bring back to a boil, uncovered. In a small bowl, combine one-and-one-half teaspoons cornstarch and one tablespoon cold water. Add the cornstarch mixture to the berries and continue to cook gently until slightly thickened, about five minutes. Transfer to a glass bowl to cool, then refrigerate.

PICNIC SPREAD MONTANA STYLE

Drape your blanket over a fallen tree — a natural backrest for a fragrant bed of soft pine needles. Two place settings snuggled side by side on your Native American banquette make your campside picnic picture perfect. Place a whole grilled trout on each plate, surrounded by a ring of squash wheels, and one or two corn muffins to perch on the rim. Spoon the berry stew into goblets for dessert.

GUELL PARK FIESTA

Olive and Bell Pepper Paste, Cilantro Shrimp,

Pimiento Rice, and Mushrooms Ajillo Tapas

Gaudí Fruit Mosaic

Sangría Blanca

Inspired by Barcelona's incredible Güell Park, compose a lively buffet of sensational Spanish *tapas* — irresistible "little dishes." Spread crusty slices of bread generously with olives and bell pepper while you pick and choose from cilantro-sauced shrimp, garlicky mushrooms, and piquant pimiento rice salad. A mosaic of fruits is a dessert tribute to the fabulous Gaudí architecture that surrounds you.

PREPARATION TIMES
The Day Before — One Hour Plus
Picnic Day — Fifteen Minutes

THE DAY BEFORE

Prepare the Olive and Bell Pepper Paste: Mix all the ingredients together, cover, and refrigerate overnight.

Prepare the Cilantro Shrimp: Toss the cooked shrimp in the cilantro pesto, cover, and refrigerate overnight.

Prepare the Pimiento Rice: Combine the pimiento dressing with the cooked rice. Cover and refrigerate overnight.

Prepare the Mushrooms Ajillo: Cover and refrigerate overnight to allow the garlicky richness of the flavors to develop.

Prepare the Fruit Mosaic: Cover and refrigerate overnight to allow the sliced fruits to macerate.

For the Sangría Blanca: Combine all the ingredients in a pitcher. Cover and refrigerate overnight.

Assemble the Picnic Basket: To serve your fiesta as they would in a Catalan taverna, pack four traditional terra-cotta *tapas* dishes and two hand-blown wine goblets. Huge, roughly hewn napkins and pretty earthenware dinner plates will give your settings a Spanish *olé*. In addition to your two sets of flatware, include three serving spoons, a spreading knife, and a dessert platter for the fruit. Have a thermos ready to transport the chilled sangría.

OLIVE AND BELL PEPPER PASTE

Broil one small yellow bell pepper until blistered on all sides. Transfer to a plastic bag for ten minutes to loosen the skin. Remove the skin and seeds, and mince the pepper. Place in a small glass bowl along with its juices. Pit and chop Spanish olives, one-quarter cup black and one-quarter cup green. Combine with the peppers. Boil two whole garlic cloves for thirty seconds. Peel, mince, and add to the olives and peppers. Rinse and chop two teaspoons capers, and add to the ingredients in the bowl. Using a fork, mix and mash together. Add just enough extra-virgin olive oil to moisten the paste (about one tablespoon). On the day of the picnic, slice a small crusty bread to spread the paste on.

CILANTRO SHRIMP

In a large pot, bring two-and-one-half quarts of water and one bay leaf to a boil. Add two garlic cloves. Blanch for thirty seconds and remove with a slotted spoon. Set aside. Place ten medium shrimp, in their shells, into the boiling water. Immediately remove the pot from the heat. Cook the shrimp until pink and firm, three to four minutes. Drain, peel, and devein the warm shrimp. Set aside in a medium bowl.

In a food processor or blender, finely chop one cup cilantro leaves with the garlic. Add one-quarter cup blanched whole almonds and process until very finely chopped. Add one-quarter cup olive oil and process until smooth. Taste for salt. Toss the cilantro pesto over the shrimp to coat.

Pimiento Rice

Bring one cup of water and a pinch of saffron to a boil in a small saucepan. Add one-quarter teaspoon salt and one-half cup long-grain rice. Simmer, covered, until tender, about fifteen minutes.

In a medium glass bowl, mix one-quarter cup olive oil, one teaspoon Dijon mustard, one tablespoon sherry vinegar, two minced green onions (green tops included), and one-quarter cup chopped pimientos. Drain the rice and add, still warm, to the bowl. Toss to coat. Taste for salt and pepper.

Mushrooms Ajillo

In a sauté pan over medium-low heat, soften two peeled minced garlic cloves in two tablespoons olive oil. Add one-half pound small mushrooms, one bay leaf, two whole cloves, and three black peppercorns. Sauté for two minutes, stirring. Add one-quarter cup white Rioja wine, one-and-one-half tablespoons fresh lemon juice, and one-quarter teaspoon salt. Cover and simmer until the mushrooms can be pierced with a fork, about five minutes. Remove the lid and raise the heat, reducing the juices to a glaze on the mushrooms. Transfer to a bowl to cool, then discard the peppercorns and cloves. Season to taste with freshly ground black pepper.

Gaudi Fruit Mosaic

Wash and dry a kaleidoscope of sun-ripened fruits, just enough for two: Valencia oranges, ruby grapes, black plums, verdant pears, blush apricots.

Slice large fruits like oranges and pears into quarters, and halve those like plums and apricots. Grapes are perfect as they are, of course. Keep the peels on: You want to retain as many colors as you can for your final presentation. Layer the fruits in a covered container, sprinkling each layer with a little sherry.

SANGRIA BLANCA

In a ceramic pitcher, combine one bottle of dry white Rioja, one-half cup Triple Sec, and a scant one-quarter cup sugar. Stir until the sugar dissolves. Thinly slice half a Valencia orange, half a lemon, and half a lime. Add to the pitcher. At the picnic site, splash in a ten-ounce bottle of club soda, if you prefer your sangría spritzed.

PICNIC SPREAD SPANISH STYLE

Select a sunny spot on the mosaic serpentine with spectacular views of the park and the turquoise waters of the Mediterranean in the distance. Arrange the *tapas* on individual dishes, to be dallied over buffet style along with an intoxicating glass of sangría. Display the multicolored fruits on the dessert platter, juxtaposing them artistically to make the vibrant Gaudí Fruit Mosaic. Spoon a little of the zippy juice over all for extra punch.

BOSTON COMMON BUFFET

Back Bay Scallop Platter

Provincetown Potato Salad

Honey-Laced Lemonade

Spiced Apple Blondies

Kick off your loafers and enjoy a picnic in the nation's first public park. Here's a buffet of all-American favorites. Broiled and thinly sliced scallops are spiced piquant and served cold in a refreshing chive-accented salad. Old-fashioned potato salad and honey-dipped lemonade make patriotic partners for the gorgeous chocolatey apple blondies.

PREPARATION TIMES
The Day Before — One Hour
Picnic Day — Five Minutes

THE DAY BEFORE

Prepare the Scallop Platter: Toss the broiled scallops in the marinade. Cover and refrigerate overnight. Wash and dry the lettuce, roll in paper towels, and refrigerate overnight in a plastic bag.

Prepare the Potato Salad: Toss the boiled potatoes to combine with the rest of the ingredients. Cover and refrigerate overnight.

Prepare the Honey-Laced Lemonade: Cover and refrigerate overnight. Wrap the lemon slices in plastic and refrigerate overnight.

Prepare the Apple Blondies: Bake the blondies. Let them sit, uncovered, at room temperature overnight.

Assemble the Picnic Basket: Wave the flag with a red, white, and blue color scheme. A comfy quilt — nothing too precious — transforms itself into a historic tablecloth. Oversized star-spangled napkins make perfect swaddling for your flatware, a pair of tumblers, and a couple of serving spoons. Include a platter for the scallops, a bowl for the potato salad, and two dinner plates. Have a thermos ready for transporting your chilled lemonade.

Back Bay Scallop Platter

8 ounces sea scallops
1/3 cup light olive oil, plus a little extra for broiling
Salt and white pepper to taste
1 cup cherry tomatoes, halved
2 tablespoons chopped chives
2 teaspoons freshly squeezed lime juice
1 1/2 teaspoons Dijon mustard
1 small shallot, peeled and minced
1 small avocado
Boston lettuce leaves

Preheat the broiler. Lightly brush the scallops with olive oil and sprinkle with salt and pepper. Place on a baking tray five inches from the heat. Broil about one minute on each side. Keep an eye on them; they cook quickly. Remove from the baking tray and allow to cool, about five minutes. Slice the scallops into one-eighth-inch pieces. Place in a glass bowl and toss with the cherry tomatoes and chives.

In a small bowl, whisk the one-third cup olive oil, lime juice, mustard, and shallot. Pour the dressing over the scallops and tomatoes. Toss to combine. Taste for salt and pepper.

On the day of the picnic, peel, seed, and dice the avocado into half-inch cubes. Toss into the scallop salad.

PROVINCETOWN POTATO SALAD

Boil one pound red-skinned potatoes until they pierce easily with a fork, about twenty minutes. Drain and cool. Peel and cut into half-inch cubes. In a glass bowl, toss the potato pieces, one small peeled, diced onion, and two tablespoons white vinegar. Add two diced celery stalks, one-half cup mayonnaise, and one-half teaspoon crushed celery seeds. Mix together gently and taste for salt and pepper.

HONEY-LACED LEMONADE

Boil four cups of water and one-half cup honey in a small saucepan. Turn down the heat and simmer, about three minutes. Remove from the heat and add three-quarters cup freshly squeezed lemon juice. Strain the cooled lemonade into a quart-size pitcher. Slice a lemon for garnish.

At the picnic site, garnish each glass with thin slices of lemon.

SPICED APPLE BLONDIES

3/4 cup all-purpose flour
1/4 teaspoon ground cinnamon
1/8 teaspoon ground nutmeg
1/8 teaspoon salt
4 ounces unsalted butter, softened
3/4 cup firmly packed light brown sugar
1 extra-large egg

1 teaspoon vanilla extract
1 large Granny Smith apple, cored and coarsely chopped
1/3 cup coarsely chopped pecans
4 ounces white chocolate, coarsely chopped

Preheat the oven to 350°F. Grease and lightly flour an eight-inch square oven-to-table baking pan. In a medium bowl, sift together the flour, cinnamon, nutmeg, and salt. Using an electric mixer, or by hand in a large bowl, beat the butter and sugar until pale and creamy. Beat in the egg, then the vanilla extract. At a low speed, beat in the spiced flour until *just* combined. Fold in the apple, pecans, and chocolate. Pour the batter into the pan.

Bake until the top is golden and a toothpick inserted in the center comes out clean, twenty-five to thirty minutes. Cool in the pan, then cut into sixteen two-inch squares.

Picnic Spread New England Style

Line your serving platter with lettuce leaves and top with the tasty sliced scallops. Pile high the potato salad in a bowl and decant the lemonade into a cut-crystal pitcher. The apple and white chocolate blondies are so deliciously tempting you had better call in the reinforcements if you want to protect your share!

Montego Bay Sun Splash

Blue Mountain Pork Tenderloin

Banana-Cucumber Raita

Spice Island Black Bean and Corn Salad

Tropical Fruit Cooler

Picnic day in the Caribbean is a sunburst of flavors. Fork-tender roast pork, juicy with gingered pineapple, is accompanied by a sprightly black bean salad and a raita refresco of bananas and cucumbers. Fruits macerated with West Indies rum come tropically presented in melon trenchers.

PREPARATION TIMES
The Day Before — One Hour Plus
Picnic Day — Twenty-Five Minutes

41

THE DAY BEFORE

For the Pork Tenderloin: Blend the ginger, onion, and garlic to a paste in a food processor. Add all the remaining ingredients and combine. Trim the pork of fat, pierce on all sides with a fork, and place in a plastic bag. Add the marinade and seal the bag securely. Give the bag a good shake to coat the loin completely. Store in the refrigerator overnight.

Prepare the Banana-Cucumber Raita: Combine all of the ingredients, except the banana. Cover and refrigerate overnight.

Prepare the Black Bean and Corn Salad: Toss to combine all the ingredients. Cover and refrigerate overnight.

Prepare the Fruit Cooler: Wrap the melon shells in plastic. Store the sliced fruits in a covered bowl. Store the mango purée in a sealed container. Refrigerate overnight.

Assemble the Picnic Basket: Mix and mismatch wildly colorful linens, polished coconut flatware, and painted crockery dinner plates in a calypso of island hues. A beach pail filled with cracked ice will make a cool-mahn cooler for some ginger beer. Don't forget your beach umbrella!

Blue Mountain Pork Tenderloin

1/2 inch fresh ginger, peeled
1/2 medium onion, peeled
2 garlic cloves, peeled
1/2 teaspoon ground cumin
3 tablespoons frozen pineapple juice concentrate
1 tablespoon fresh mint leaves
1 tablespoon olive oil
1/8 teaspoon salt
1 small pork tenderloin, 1 pound or less

Preheat the oven to 375°F. Remove the pork loin from the marinade, discarding the marinade. Place in a roasting pan and roast until a meat thermometer registers 145°F, fifteen to twenty minutes. Let the loin cool, then cut it into thin slices.

Banana-Cucumber Raita

In a medium bowl, mix eight ounces of plain yogurt, one tablespoon lemon juice, one tablespoon chopped fresh cilantro, and a dash of salt and freshly ground black pepper until smooth. Stir in one peeled, seeded, and diced cucumber.

On the day of the picnic, peel and dice one ripe, but firm, banana. Fold into the raita and taste for salt and pepper.

Spice Island Black Bean and Corn Salad

1 cup black beans, cleaned and rinsed
1 onion, peeled and roughly chopped
1 1/4 cups corn kernels, fresh or frozen
1/2 teaspoon ground cumin
1/2 teaspoon ground coriander
1/2 teaspoon dried oregano, crumbled
1 tablespoon red wine vinegar
1/4 teaspoon salt
Freshly ground black pepper to taste
1/4 cup olive oil
1/4 cup chopped fresh cilantro

Place the beans in a covered medium saucepan, cover with cold water, and bring to a boil. Boil for one minute. Remove from the heat and let stand for one hour. Drain the beans, discard the water, and begin again by covering the beans with fresh water. Add the onion. Bring to a boil and simmer, uncovered, until the beans are tender, about forty-five minutes. Drain the beans and set aside in a large glass bowl.

Blanch the corn in a small pan of boiling water for one minute. Drain, rinse, and add to the beans. Toss well.

Dry-toast the cumin, coriander, and oregano in a small skillet over low heat until they give off a warm, fragrant aroma. Transfer the spices to a small glass bowl. Stir in the vinegar, salt, and pepper to taste. Whisk in the olive oil, then the cilantro. Pour the dressing over the beans and corn and toss well to combine. Taste again for salt and pepper.

TROPICAL FRUIT COOLER

Cut one small ripe cantaloupe in half, remove the seeds, and scoop out the flesh. Set aside the shells for serving the cooler. Dice the melon flesh into one-inch cubes. Set aside in a bowl. Rinse and hull one cup strawberries. Slice each in half. Add to the cantaloupe. Peel one ripe mango. Dice into one-inch cubes. Toss half the mango cubes with the cantaloupe and strawberries. Purée the remainder in a blender with two teaspoons lime juice and two teaspoons dark Jamaican rum. Set aside in a bowl.

On the day of the picnic, pour the purée over the fruits and gently toss together to combine.

PICNIC SPREAD JAMAICAN STYLE

A lovely table accent is the lush frangipani flowers that grow everywhere in wild tangles. Layer slices of pork along the center of each dinner plate, flanking the succulent meat with portions of black bean salad and refreshing raita. Spoon a hearty helping of diced fruit into the hollow centers of the melon trenchers and top tartly with mango purée. Pop the stopper on some ginger beer and get with the native rhythm of a Jamaican sun splash.

VILLA BORGHESE INTERMEZZO

Tricolor Roasted Peppers with Mozzarella Fresca

Pollo alla Diavolo

Amor Polenta Cake with Fresh Strawberries

Chilled Frascati Wine

Picnic Italian style is a Roman menu enjoyed alfresco. As sounds of the city rise from the crowded cafés along the Via Veneto, sip a *bicchiere* of tart Frascati. Munch on grilled chicken spiced "hot as the devil," accompanied by a succulent salad of smoky peppers and fresh mozzarella. The Amor Polenta Cake served with fresh strawberries is surely a taste of *la dolce vita.*

PREPARATION TIMES
The Day Before — One Hour
Picnic Day — Thirty-Five Minutes

THE DAY BEFORE

Prepare the Roasted Peppers: Cover and refrigerate overnight to allow the full richness of the flavors to maturate the peppers.

For the Pollo alla Diavolo: Prepare the marinade by combining all of the ingredients in a small nonaluminum baking dish. Wash and dry the chicken pieces. Remove most of the skin and all of the fat. Cut three vertical slits down to the bone on both sides of each piece. Turn the chicken in the marinade to cover, spooning the juices into the slits. Cover and refrigerate overnight.

Prepare the Amor Polenta Cake with Fresh Strawberries: Bake the cake. Let it sit, uncovered, at room temperature overnight. Rinse the strawberries and pat off the moisture. Leave them to dry thoroughly so they don't become mushy during the night. Cover and refrigerate overnight.

Assemble the Picnic Basket: Pack a black-and-white checkered tablecloth, wrapping your flatware in matching napkins. For a real Roman holiday, take along red, white, and green dishes, including a cake plate, a pair of wineglasses, and a corkscrew. On the day of the picnic, carry the wine in a tightly closed plastic bag, half filled with ice cubes, to keep the bottle chilled until you are ready to enjoy it.

TRICOLOR ROASTED PEPPERS WITH MOZZARELLA FRESCA

3 bell peppers (1 red, 1 green, and 1 yellow)
1/4 cup extra-virgin olive oil
Splash of balsamic vinegar to taste
2 anchovies, minced
1 garlic clove, peeled and crushed
Salt and freshly ground black pepper to taste
1/4 pound fresh mozzarella, grated

Preheat the broiler. Place the peppers on a cookie sheet and grill on all sides until charred. Transfer the peppers to a plastic bag and sweat for about ten minutes. Peel off the skins, remove the stems and seeds, and discard. Do not rinse. Tear the roasted peppers into one-half-inch strips.

In a small glass bowl, combine the olive oil, vinegar, anchovies, garlic, salt, and pepper. Line the bottom of a small terra-cotta au gratin dish with the pepper strips, alternating red, green, and yellow. Spoon the dressing over all to cover. Sprinkle the grated mozzarella around the sides of the dish to ring the peppers.

POLLO ALLA DIAVOLO

Juice of 2 lemons, freshly squeezed (about 1/3 cup)
2 tablespoons olive oil
1 1/2 teaspoons coarse ground black pepper, plus a few
     grindings of fresh black pepper

2 tablespoons finely chopped fresh mint leaves
1/2 teaspoon salt
4 to 6 chicken pieces (legs and thighs)

Preheat the grill or broiler. Remove the chicken from the marinade. Grill skin side down, about fifteen minutes. Baste often with the marinade. Turn the chicken over and continue to grill for another fifteen minutes, still basting faithfully.

Amor Polenta Cake with Fresh Strawberries

2/3 cup unsalted butter, at room temperature
1 cup confectioners' sugar, sifted, plus a little for dusting
1 teaspoon vanilla extract
2 eggs, plus 1 yolk
1 1/4 cups cake flour
1/2 cup yellow cornmeal
10 fresh strawberries

Preheat the oven to 325°F. Butter a four-cup loaf pan and dust with flour. Using an electric mixer, or by hand in a large bowl, beat the butter and sugar together until pale and creamy. Beat in the vanilla extract. Stir in the eggs, one at a time, incorporating each fully before adding the next. Beat in the flour, and then the cornmeal. Beat until the mixture is *just* combined. The batter should retain a coarse texture. Pour the batter into the prepared pan. Bake until a toothpick inserted in the center comes out clean, forty to forty-five minutes. Let the cake cool in the pan for ten minutes, then unmold it onto a cooling rack. Do not force it out of the pan. Try again later if it doesn't come out easily at first.

On the day of the picnic, dust the top with confectioners' sugar.

Picnic Spread Italian Style

Spread your tablecloth under a tall cypress and strew ivy vines here and there for decoration. Unwrap the flatware and reroll the napkins, tying them with a length of curling ivy. While you take your first sip of pleasantly chilled wine, place two pieces of Pollo alla Diavolo on each dinner plate. Arrange slices of Tricolor Roasted Peppers and Mozzarella alongside, drizzling a little tangy dressing on top. Surround the Amor Polenta Cake with the ripe strawberries for a *pranzo molto bene.*

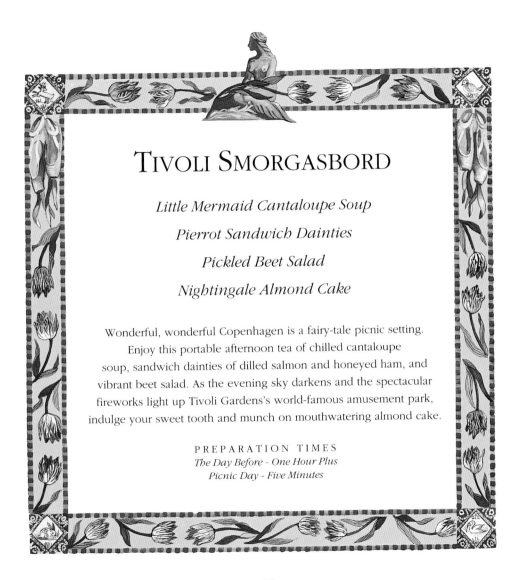

TIVOLI SMORGASBORD

Little Mermaid Cantaloupe Soup

Pierrot Sandwich Dainties

Pickled Beet Salad

Nightingale Almond Cake

Wonderful, wonderful Copenhagen is a fairy-tale picnic setting.
Enjoy this portable afternoon tea of chilled cantaloupe
soup, sandwich dainties of dilled salmon and honeyed ham, and
vibrant beet salad. As the evening sky darkens and the spectacular
fireworks light up Tivoli Gardens's world-famous amusement park,
indulge your sweet tooth and munch on mouthwatering almond cake.

PREPARATION TIMES
The Day Before - One Hour Plus
Picnic Day - Five Minutes

The Day Before

Prepare the Cantaloupe Soup: Blend all the ingredients together. Pour into a thermos and refrigerate overnight to allow the flavors to meld.

Prepare the Sandwich Dainties: Store the eight sandwiches in the refrigerator overnight.

Prepare the Beet Salad: Toss the julienned beets in the dressing to marinate. Cover and refrigerate overnight.

Prepare the Almond Cake: Bake the cake. Let it sit, uncovered, at room temperature overnight.

Assemble the Picnic Basket: In the folds of a lace tablecloth, carefully wrap two Copenhagen blue serving plates, two dessert plates, and two small salad plates for offering the succulent pickled beets. The melon soup will taste best sipped from wide-rimmed tea cups. Roll your forks in napkins trimmed with sea-blue ribbon, and include a serving spoon and serrated cake knife.

Little Mermaid Cantaloupe Soup

Peel and seed one ripe cantaloupe. Cut into one-inch cubes. Purée the cubes in a blender, one third at a time, until smooth. Add one-half cup plain yogurt and blend. Add one-half cup chicken stock, one tablespoon freshly squeezed lime juice, and a pinch of freshly grated nutmeg. Blend well. Taste for salt and pepper.

Pierrot Sandwich Dainties

In a food processor, beat four tablespoons of unsalted butter until light and fluffy. Add six ounces smoked salmon and process thoroughly. Add one teaspoon freshly squeezed lemon juice, one tablespoon rinsed capers, and two teaspoons freshly minced dill, processing each separately until evenly blended. Grind in a few hearty twists of the pepper mill to taste. Set the salmon spread aside.

Remove the crusts from four slices of light rye bread. Run a rolling pin over each slice to make the bread malleable and easy to roll. Spread one quarter of the dilled salmon on each slice of bread. Roll each sandwich up, being careful not to tear the bread. Seal each sandwich in plastic wrap to keep it tightly rolled.

In a small bowl, combine one-quarter cup Dijon mustard and one-and-one-half tablespoons honey. Set aside. Remove the crusts from four slices of dark rye and roll out as before. Spread an even layer of honeyed mustard on each slice of bread. Place one thin slice of honey-baked Danish ham on each slice of bread, trimming the ham to fit. Using a cheese plane, thinly slice four ounces of Danbo cheese. Place a single layer of cheese atop each slice of ham. Roll each sandwich up tightly and seal in plastic wrap.

Pickled Beet Salad

Trim one bunch of beets (about six small tubers), leaving an inch of the tops intact. Wash well and place in a medium saucepan. Cover with two inches of water and bring to a boil. Lower the heat and simmer, covered, until the beets can be pierced with the tip of a knife, about forty minutes. Drain. When the beets are cool enough to handle, slip off the skins and discard them. Cut the beets into half-inch strips and set aside.

In a glass bowl, whisk one tablespoon cider vinegar, one teaspoon sugar, one tablespoon green peppercorn mustard, two tablespoons olive oil, two tablespoons chopped fresh chives, and salt and freshly ground black pepper to taste. Dress the julienned beets and toss.

Nightingale Almond Cake

8 ounces almond paste
4 ounces unsalted butter, at room temperature
3/4 cup sugar
3 large eggs, at room temperature
1/4 teaspoon almond extract
1 tablespoon kirsch
1/4 cup all-purpose flour
1/2 teaspoon baking powder

Preheat the oven to 350°F. Using an electric mixer, or by hand in a large bowl, beat the almond paste and butter until creamy. Beat in the sugar.

Beat in the eggs, one at a time, mixing thoroughly before adding the next egg. Beat in the almond extract and kirsch. Beat in the flour and baking powder until the mixture is *just* combined. Do not overmix or the cake will collapse in the center. Butter an eight-inch round cake pan and dust with flour. Pour the batter into the pan and bake until a toothpick inserted in the center comes out clean, about thirty-five minutes. Let the cake cool in the pan for thirty minutes. Then invert it onto a rack to cool completely.

Picnic Spread Danish Style

Since it's a Copenhagen Gardens tradition, rent a lakeside table at Tivoli's charming turn-of-the-century café. Arrange your platter of sandwich dainties in a diamond pattern, alternating dark and light rye, to create a harlequin effect in honor of dear Pierrot. Garnish with delicate fronds of fragrant dill to enhance your lacy table settings. Begin with a teacup of chilled melon soup and a small salad plate of juicy beet salad. Thin slivers of rich almond cake make a happy ending.